PEARLS BENEATH
THE RIND

by

Richard Seldin

and

Carole R Seldin-Bolinski

First published by Dog Ear Publishing
4010 W. 86th Street, Ste H
Indianapolis, IN 46268
www.dogearpublishing.net

ISBN: 978-1-4575-2210-9

This book is printed on acid-free paper.

Printed in the United States of America

PREFACE

$\mathcal{S}$ ome ten years ago my sister, Carole, asked me to collaborate on a book of poems. Although my mind initially flashed the response "I'm not interested," for several seconds I hesitated to answer. To be fair there were practical reasons for not immediately responding. I hadn't written any new poems in awhile and was very involved with my career as a Federal Government attorney. Perhaps the more important reason for my hesitancy, however, was the counterweight it allowed to deal with a negative reaction to suggestions of my sister, a reaction that was as old as she was.

As I saw it, Carole and I had grown up as hostile rivals in a family that was emotionally battered and bruised beyond most. I recall us going off to summer "brother and sister" camps when I was 11, and Carole 7, and being required to attend weekly Sunday afternoon gatherings for siblings. Although these brother and sister encounters probably lasted no more than an hour, they still seemed endless. During this ordeal I would notice how much fun some of my friends appeared to be having with their little sisters or brothers, and wondered whether they were faking it. Why couldn't I feel the affection they seemed to be expressing to each other? Was there something wrong with me or with them? At that age I wasn't sure of the answer, but was aware of my envy about the difference.

Fortunately, my hesitancy about responding to Carole's idea about a book proved valuable because it allowed for other possibilities: the endeavor might not only prove to be stimulating and entertaining and result in resurrecting a number of poems I felt were reasonably good, but would allow us to cooperate on a project of interest to both of us.

One mystery remained: how did Carole know I'd written any poems she'd want to put in a book with hers? This was due to a remarkable coincidence. Without having the slightest knowledge of the other's efforts, several years before she and I had entered a poem in the same amateur poetry competition. When she was asked to edit her poem for the contest and subsequent publication in the volume, a computer hit for the name "Seldin" produced a "Seldin", who much to her surprise wasn't her, but rather her brother. Although I knew Carole was writing fiction, I'd assumed the last poetry she'd written was in high school; and though she was aware I'd earlier written a few short stories, I didn't remember telling her I'd written poems as well. When she called to tell me about finding my poem, I laughed at this bizarre occurrence; partly a laugh at having been caught red-handed entering a vanity, amateur poetry contest, but mostly a big guffaw that truly reflected my surprise. Nevertheless, after we read each other's contest poems, we put our poetry back in their individual boxes, and moved on without comment or further sharing of our efforts. As I recall, the most we offered about our entries was "nice poem" as if we were back in high school describing a bland date.

The next real talk about poems came several years later, during the course of our father's terminal illness when Carole asked me if I'd written any poems about him, and if I had, whether I would send them to her. It turned out that I had written one, "Pa"—not in this collection—which described some of the flash-points in my relationship with our father. Although initially I was reluctant to share it, mostly because I thought it more of a jingle than a poem, the desire to convey some of my feelings about him proved stronger, and finally I did send it on. On the other hand, I didn't volunteer the poem, "Family Visit"—included in this collection—which described the frustration and despair I felt during and after family gatherings, including earlier visits with Carole.

After I agreed with Carole to compile the collection we have titled "Pearls Beneath The Rind" and first read her contributions, I was struck by a number of similarities in our poems, notably the frequent use of relatively short lines, irregular rhyme, strong rhythm and a song-like quality. Despite these likenesses, after several readings I became more impressed by their pronounced differences. Though there are exceptions, Carole's poems tend to focus on the outer world and often on a particular place in that world even when depicting relationships. A number are so visually compelling they could easily be turned into paintings. In contrast, my focus is on the play of the mind, either in exploring a thought or idea or in describing a relationship. As a result, my work often employs self-referential, conversational and dream-like states and rarely mentions place in any detail. Also, when depicting relationships, Carole's poems tend to describe aspects of the lengthy involvements she has had; whereas mine, due, in part, to the time when they were written, evoke the searching world of the single and the delights and disappointments that accompany brief affairs.

These profound differences in our work shouldn't have come as a surprise. As siblings go, Carole and I are quite different in character and have lived vastly different lives in different places. The reader might well ask why we would want to co-author a book of poems that doesn't depict our relationship as brother and sister, and says nothing about sibling relationships in general. For me, one answer is our keen interest in poetry and a mutual desire to share with readers how two siblings have used it to express their separate worlds. But a larger purpose is to celebrate a collaboration made possible through an evolving loving relationship which we had no access to as children and young adults. In this sense our book affirms that even heavily conflicted sibling relationships can substantially improve.

Richard Seldin

*W*hen I was growing up I felt invisible and the only communication I remember were reprimands from my parents. Although I knew my brother was around, I kept away from him because 1) our age difference, 4 years, seemed like a light year and 2) he represented the adult world that was always mixed up in my view. It wasn't until I was at an age when my brother started dating some of my friends that I took a closer look at what he was doing with his life and started to embrace some of his beliefs. Because I revered him, I was truly surprised to find out how much my presence really bothered him. But that was after the fact, and I didn't see it as a young girl. After becoming more immersed in the world and how I could get along in it, I found that my brother's beliefs were not mine, and that created a stumbling block in our relationship. As I pulled away from everyone, he moved closer to family.

Left to work on my own demons, I had very little contact with my brother, although I do remember him visiting me in Arizona. It was our father's illness and death that put a different perspective on family for me. Since our mother had died a number of years before, now that my brother and I were "orphans", it made the idea of holding onto family and getting over the muck that we once carried easier to put aside, particularly since neither of us had children. Facing mortality alone seemed like a bad idea. Besides, with my brother's influence, I was learning how to enjoy and understand why he saw things the way he did.

When we first started our book it was called, *Along The Way*, and had a number of other poems which I made into a chapbook, and sent it on to him for his birthday. Perhaps my brother saw possibilities because after doing the chapbook, we became more serious. I replaced a number of my poems with newer ones while my brother edited many of his and deleted others. A few times we came close to dropping the project, but when that happened, one of us wanted to keep it alive.

"Pearls Beneath The Rind" gave my brother and I the opportunity to reunite.

Carole R Seldin-Bolinski

TABLE OF CONTENTS

INNER SANCTUM
Richard Seldin

IF YOU OPENED MY SKIN
Carole R Seldin-Bolinski

TABLE OF CONTENTS

THE TOUCH
Richard Seldin

TIME STRETCHES LIKE BUBBLE GUM
Carole R Seldin-Bolinski

TABLE OF CONTENTS

NIGHTSONGS
Richard Seldin

"After the sibling, nothing is the same again."

—Juliet Mitchell in *Siblings*

INNER SANCTUM

It Was A Point Of Light

that couldn't be denied;
growing, as slowly as my age,
or had been there all along, unseen.

It was nonchalant, effortless,
as spontaneous as space,
as radiant as radiant is.

Just a small point, mind you, and
best unadorned
by poetic abstractions;
yet, still it was there,
illumining my being.

A Quiet Night

Some nights are just quiet.
They appear to say nothing do nothing feel nothing,
are mostly lost in a drifting cloud.

Yet these languid moments
can be deceptive: also hungering
like a rat's fang dripping
with the latest quash.

By this I mean, from
point-to-point, we're talking galaxy:
on one end, a bump on a log,
and, at the other, behold—
a bungee jump rhyme.

Frankly

So what if your dull sigh
lacks the wind
to force a thump.
It's only Monday.
Tuesday could be a day
of ripe plums; Wednesday
a lottery win; Thursday a new love,
and Friday a larkish bath.
Which is to say that
sitting here waiting for
better times,
frankly,
is a drag.

Waiting For The Word

It seems everything is moving
only from the outside out
and not from the inside out
or even the outside in. So that
lines drop like sand bags on a bare floor:
as useless as warmed over seaweed; actually
not even that which is unique.

I sit at my desk thinking about
air bags fitting on airheads
and breathe in a rush of clichés.
"You're supposed to show, not tell"
is the purpose *ex cathedra*.
But I've got a fish that stews pedagogical,
a lectern hanging from its gills.

Well, tomorrow is another day.
Maybe I can try the soaps for inspiration,
or hunt grizzles.

Baptism

I learned what baptism is,
the other day,
in the shower.
Cascading streams of water
rolling over the shoulder:
the knot in the gut is gone,
the monkey's whine perishes.

Was the idea
to clean out the pores,
the gaping holes
where no roses grew
so they could grow?

Quickly picked up as hype
by the sandcastle and dry bones types—
and off the party went
down the star struck millennia,
drowning in meanings.

Until finally,
in that same shower,
water became water again.

A Night's Spark

Tonight I want to ride the rail
full speed on,
breathe in corn and honeysuckle.
Tonight I want to woof up slopes, straddle eaves
and delight in the bread of it.
Like a holy place at dawn and empty—
all mine to do with.

To tell a tale pungent
as a Cuban stogie,
a louche singles bar;
that would be a rage no matter the age.

Yet, after all the years of inner sleuthing—
the messenger now snoring in my ear—
even when aloft
I can't hold it.
This red shifting spark
already fraying beyond the edge.

Progress

Progress over time, what is it?
The work award the name
in the press on the tube
stocks soaring election
marriage the family?

Or is it the difference between
preoccupation with the literal fact
and movement beyond
the literal fact,
which still shows concern
for the fact, but
not with its literalness?

Last week
a friend reminded me
I'd forgotten where we'd played tennis
three weeks before.
I remembered the tennis
but not the place.
Two years ago this could not
have happened. My mind
could not have ignored place.

When he was alive
my father and I spoke by phone
every two weeks, alternating
who called whom.
For years I could never forget
whose turn it was to call.
But then something happened,
something like a warm, cleansing sponge
got in the way,
so that I no longer remembered the sequence
and occasionally forgot the week.

Progress (continued)

Some people claim
this difference in the
pressure of the mind is more significant
than career wealth
certain varieties of love—
all of the above.
The more bold suggest
it inhibits the common cold.
While I'm inclined to agree,
this still needs working out.

Saturday Afternoon

It used to be that the
putsching mink of ambition
pressed on me so hard
there was no space
between impulse and action,
so that I dove full in,
a glutton to all I could do
to be prince.

But lately an ebbing
has been occurring,
so that the hunger
for spoils to take from the world
has drawn back some,
urgency, yet also commitment, lost.

Thus, I sit wondering,
whether I've moved on, as one does,
or whether real possibilities have waned
through age and accommodation.

The Pantheon

The titans flash by,
those of my pantheon.
In smooth unbound flight
they soar to unreachable heights;
and even when crashing
splatter gloriously on shore.

If they would only
stand up the size of men;
hum an off-key tune
at break of day;
take off
for a quick bite
at noon;
also blow a nose when cold.

I try to draw the titans away,
move them this way and that,
blink them on and off.
But they're too big in me:
I can't leave them.

Windmills For Sigmund

The days jerk by
in rhythms I cannot exactly choose.
Appearing, disappearing,
a run of angular riffs,
notes that jar
yet echo the source.
While the messenger, perched on leather, ruminating,
listens for connections.

This is one mode
of the inner sanctum.
What is
and what will be
are so preternaturally similar
to what was.
"History is bunk"?
An idiot's bark
over a land featuring spin
by the millisecond
and fifty varieties of vaginal spray,
to flee it.

To know this is a problem,
to feel this is a problem,
provides little surcease.
Our formulations proliferate and die
like flies on violent neon.

We've been around the block,
around and around the block.
We've rammed the block,
we've hammered the block
but the block is relentless.

Chipping away to make the block unblock is fine.
One might say it's the only way that counts.
But time and space are limited.
Perhaps nitro is preferable,
or a laser.

Family Visit

There are few mysteries,
really. Mostly the revival
of old scores,
bludgeoning precarious
attempts to live a life,
so that the usual
traversing of the thin edge
quickly segues
into heavy metal.

You could have predicted it too,
before the visit.
My brain's screen
fecund with what would be,
raising a slew
of diversionary actions and hows to control.

And then, of course, the show, as it was.
Watching up close the ride
I've been so often on before
and thought ridded of.
To reason it away,
feel it away,
hit up the messenger for a fix:
as apt as sugar on a blaze.
As if I wanted it all
in place of love.

So that in the aftermath,
strewn with shards,
all that's left is
further explanation.

IF YOU OPENED MY SKIN

Intended

Although I intended to love
with breath of butterfly
and length of anaconda,
with heart of devoted dog
and hope of young child,

I have loved
with breath of skunk
and length of ant,
with heart of jellyfish
and taste of hard soil.

Did You Ever Hear Wind Rustle?

I can see it rustle,
trees bending in a constant back and forth.
I can feel it rustle,
a continuous breeze against
face and hair. Then up in the
air and back to tickle nose
and mouth.

I've closed my eyes and
tried to absorb its sound,
tried to smell its breath
and swallow its sighing murmurs.

But it takes a wise look into nature,
more than a quick ear
to hear wind echo, creep into
its rattle and understand its speech.

Personally,
I'd rather eat ice cream.

Skin Deep

If you opened my skin
there'd be sediments
from past loves,
a time when skin was smooth
eyes alert and wanting.

If you opened my skin
you'd find oil and acrylic paint,
charcoal and my favorite 4B
drawing pencils.
An apple for still lifes,
an imagination for everything else.

There'd be an assortment of riches,
debris that needed cleaning,
and a cobweb as thick
as night to hold them in,
if you opened my skin.

Slinging Drywall

I'm a drywall mama
slinging drywall sheets
over my shoulders
atop a drywall hoist
rolling up to vaulted ceilings
to meet joist to joist.

A drywall mama
unpacking 4x12 sheets,
stacking them in rows
to be hung at a later date,
to ensure drywall won't buckle
and will remain
ready-to-use straight.

A drywall mama,
with drywall dust
embedded in face
and hands,
in nails, cuticles, ears and hair,
falling on lips,
smelling like bread yeast.

There's always more.
More drywall to mount.
I'm like a drywall saint
always ready to hoist,
join, nail, tape,
then, finally,
ready to paint.

Bathing In Paint

I want to bathe in paint
have it travel down my leg
then back, inching up my thigh
between my legs.

It glistens in the roller pan
smooth like velvet,
wet and pliable.

I am forever awed by its thick
gloss; its lasting presence on walls,
the permanence of its dye. I want to float
in its layers, have it drip on my eyelids,
bead on my feet.

Spreading paint is
taking a ride in the country,
relaxing, with its repetition.
Up. Down. Up. Down.
Covering old mistakes,
the paint gliding like a
skater.

The paint stroke—a kiss—
the mixing and melting of paint.
It's as if a lover holds
your face in his hands,
caresses your neck and ears.
Then tells you,
I, too, love paint.

Brave Dog

My dog's energy bubbles
like percolating coffee.
She does back flips
then stops as something in the
distance breaks her concentration.
She barks, backs into
my leg.

She barks again,
her tongue red, sweating salt,
her tail ruffled wool.

She wants to welcome him
but senses I don't like
the approaching man.
So she sits, hindquarters squat,
front legs straight.
Both of us rigid
as a cemented fence post.

My dog knows the routine,
knows to stay beside me
especially
when he gets too close.
No happy wags
or mounting jumps.
Just sit, stay, and watch.

He doesn't remain long,
enough to pick up
the boxes piled
along the driveway,
his things

Brave Dog (continued)

that used to droop in the
closet, and tools that
invaded the shed.
No looking back,
no more pleading.
I don't wave goodbye.

She watches too,
her tongue unfolds to
her chin,
prevents a whine
that would break our silence,
her choice of me over him.

"Ti amo,"
words I used to say to him
are now whispered in her ear.
"Cane valoroso."
Brave dog.

Back Then

we had dogs,
tails wagging,
tongues lapping.
We were family.

It was all about
caring and sharing,
brushing dogs' teeth,
getting their shots on time,
having their warm bodies pressed close
on our bed.

Back then
we didn't realize their teeth
would rot,
we'd forget their shots
and end each day sleeping
in separate beds.

Back in the days
we had dogs
we never thought our love
would turn to obligation,
become hard,
unbending
like a stale dog treat.

Sweet Sixteen

My dreams blew
out the flickering lights—
one wish, two,
three, maybe four.

It came before long hair
and trips to Manhattan,
before tie dyes and earring holes
and the sweet bitter smells of wafting weed.
Even before the Vietnam War.

It came before Arizona,
sagebrush and prickly pear.
Before all-day jobs
elbowed in their consequences.
Even before PC's and iPods.

My sweet sixteen.
A time of changing moods
and lipsticks.
A time for naïve thoughts
and pantyhose.
A time for a young girl
to have more than a few wishes.

Bad Electricity

I remember your breath—
chamomile and licorice—
skin smell of orange peel and lemon grass,
yearning to taste sweat and salt
feel your electric fingers
surge through my body
Again.
And again.

Instead
I now lie numb against your hands
worn from cable and wire,
their cold touch on my breast and thigh.
I lie limp
counting ceiling tiles
while I listen to your snore.

And yet
through these years
of static promises,
these years of uncaring whispers,
I still wait for those words,
I love you.
I love you.

The Wedding Band

Its loop of gold doesn't wear
like other rings;
no scratches or dents
or tarnish from years of wear.

Some areas of reflected light
still beam, as if crying out
from its curved yellow mouth,
There's still another chance.

Waves Of Memories

We met in New York,
your hands of subway steel
and eyes wet with wonder.
Sharing a home on Long Island
we slept on sand dunes,
covered our bodies with ocean salt.

We moved to the desert
where our love dried out
like dead cholla branches.
Our arguments
bundled into a fireball,
yelling at anything
unimportant... like who
forgot to put the soggy cod
in the freezer, or who left the
empty milk carton in the frig.

I can stroll by any house
and still see our dreams
piled inside,
or cook a paella
and remember our walks along
the Mediterranean.

But those memories don't
linger. They ebb and flow,
turn off like a light
then wash out to sea.

Changing Seasons

Sit upon the hill with me.
Hear the cool sounds of fall
sweep across our cheeks.
Soon winter will push in,
frost our skin crimson
like the turning leaves.

Sit upon the hill with me.
Wonder at the iridescence of
a spider's web,
a soft glow
in a delicate sun.
Listen to the cicadas
their songs now staccato,
desperate for an end-of-season mate.

Sit upon the hill with me.
But don't tell me
the dog refused to eat,
your leg hurts,
or you need to buy coffee.

Tell me you care.
Tell me you had cared.
Tell me you will always care.
And if you can't tell me
these things, then

Sit upon the hill with me
one last time.

THE TOUCH

Sunday Night

Tonight I long
for your breath on my heart,
a guitar string in the wind,
to roll and tumble
in the gush
of love.

We start on a rock
at night light,
the sun glaze down
the low moon hidden.
It's startling,
how long I've searched,
it's frightening.

Then we waltz above
the cloud cover
beyond the rough,
our eyes purling teardrops.
With you:
"How our bodies fit."
And me:
"The glow, well it's here."

A short festal interval,
until a natural bridge
brings us back,
and we have Monday to consider.

April Bells

There is no denying
a fragrant windblown day in April.
Gazing out the window
with desire overrunning
on a zesty earth-blessed day in April.

With trees in midst of budding
with songbirds at their singing
with females flushed and strutting
with heartbeats wild and rushing.

There is no hesitation
such compelling palpitation
all bodies at gestation.
On a balmy sunkissed day,
a spicy golden day,
a sultry sunburst day
in April.

Round Midnight

Outside the Three Note Café,
the left bank swirled
in a foggy blue wave
to the wail of a sax
hailing fingers
that danced along ivories.

As I took in the scene,
I wondered how it would be,
again with you
beside me.

On Missing You

I put it on the back burner;
the us.
I put it on the back burner;
the tough.
To see you in a dream or
alone when I arise
is clearly not enough.
I put us on the back burner;
it's rough.

March Snow

Last night I swung
as the Orangutan might leap
from bough to bough,
up with a story of love—
a friend who'd beaten
the no in her—
and down with my own story—
a crisscross of spite and woe.

Then in the flurrying whiteness,
long before dawn,
down deeper I swung
until I entered the dream
of you.

As I woke to a curious mix
of snowdrifts and spring sun,
back up I swung,
thinking of you,
and I don't know you.

The Holy Ones

While we lunch, she says:
"Thanks for the interest
but I don't wanta
get too friendly
with guys at the office
just friendly up to a point.
Know what I mean?
I mean maybe but
let's talk later not now
not that I'm seeing anyone
in particular
on second thought no.
Know what I mean?"

Later, I visit a friend
with AIDS;
my best teacher, he dies too;
and, worse than usual
work hassles.

They who live and
bear it day after day,
they are holy ones,
the men of the east.

We Weren't Right

You recoil
at a word wrongly placed.
You frown
when I admire your face.
You laugh
to ward off an embrace.
You take offense
long before defense
is appropriate.

I know well these wonts,
being a master of rolls
and turns, bucking
long before I ride.

So that after all the chafe
your form disappears.
And I was just
beginning to like you.

Alice Variations 1

Your hair brushed
across the flat rock,
and sweeping long,
creased the mountain's side.
You were there, full and true,
filling the virgin gorge
with bolts of air.

But purple words will not do,
all that screech and scraw.
And not the terse, sensate sound
that shakes the day.

Alice Variations 4

I thought she was grand.
Embodiment of the lovely woman,
as well as a lusty, busty broad
with a brain big as a warehouse,
a voice of melted butter,
and too she'd open car doors for you.

She'd been loved by a decent number
over the foamy wave of a long youth,
including earlier the best friend,
forming multiple triads to get off on.

And like with a seasoned carnybarker—
there was always that one compelling hope
as the oval wheel rat-ta-tatted rat-ta-tatted
around nails enclosing treasures
only whales could find.

So I returned to the wheel
and played again, won again;
played again, lost again,
and so on and such
until reality became an issue,
her confessing she'd moved on;
and, for me, hinting
of other pretties waiting.

Then, like more often than not,
after a brief flash flood,
all was well and comprehended
in a logistical way,
me emitting: "I'm glad for you."
While the undertow, this time,
appeared in a fear of cancerous lungs;
and hell, I didn't even smoke.

Odd

Even the act of sitting
in the work chair,
but not working,
wishing the work done,
but not doing. Even that beats
depression, chocolate shakes,
studying Japanese.

Even the numb run
of my hand across
empty space:
spluttering, fluttering, stuttering.
Not able to compose
one solid line.
That too tops a fine French wine.

Even the fading imago
of the self's dream,
forget about contracts,
future rights, a roll on the screen.
Just a scant, distant cry.
Even that enhances
and I don't know why.

Watching A Line

The easy way is
watching a line form
as it forms;
not having a minimal idea,
let alone grand design,
but whatever comes forth
is a good.

Once writing:
"A crocodilian patter"
to describe
the whistling winter wind.
Would you believe that,
the lines one goes?

"God she was fine,
a timbre like butter."

TIME STRETCHES LIKE BUBBLE GUM

Winter In Chino Valley

I live indoors in winter,
bundled in layers
peering through my front window
for anything green, anything plucky
enough to withstand the bitter cold.

It's the time of year when gophers and tarantulas
burrow into frosted soil,
when rabbits and skunks
wrap their progeny in fur,
when my neighbor's hard-skinned cows
huddle together against the chill.

The daily scenes don't change:
naked tumbleweed gathering
in barbed clumps, icy
tree limbs bending
in the strain of winter.

A steady draft
seeps through a window crack,
blows against my cheek
as I touch the cold glass.

It tempts me to look outside again,
witness the icing on mountain tops,
crushed leaves piled in empty tree wells
and Siberian elms, like broom handles,
branching into night's sky.

The harsh stare on a horse's face,
blanketed in heavy shawls
reminds me how lucky I am
to be sheltered within.

Winter in Chino Valley (continued)

Protected from this arctic weather,
its frozen twists of air,
I meet nature indoors, on
my turf, and dissolve her
in the warmth of my winter mouth.

Next Meal

"Hey, black bird,"
I call out to raven.
He sits atop a gate post
waiting for carrion to appear.

He mimics my voice and
spreads his wings,
stripes of green iridescent bands
shimmer through daylight.

"Hey,"
I say again.
He raises his chest
and does a two-step on
the fence as he waits
for rabbit, prairie dog
and best of all,
gopher.

Raven delights in my waiting,
thinking I will attack his
meal first, like coyote or
hawk. Then he will swipe little
pieces of these daily specials.
His easiest menu comes
from dirt roads, back alleys and
properties where I roost.
First: appetizers of small bugs and seeds.
Second course: road kill.

But he and I know that the
main entrée is gopher.
His favorite dish is underground,
and he has no helpers to
kick up dirt.

Next Meal (continued)

"Black bird
I think you're a con.
I bet you do fly-bys and pick
up prey on your own,
carry them off with your talons
and fly into hidden layers of sky."

He screeches and flutters his
feathers. Maybe I saw a
bit of truth.

We watch each other,
perched on opposite
sides of a dirt road.

He flaps his wings one last time,
circles and swoops over my head
then takes off. Raven will look for
another sucker, someone or something to
open his next meal.

I'm left alone
resting on my fence,
wondering,
*Who will catch
and prepare my next meal?*

We Want To See You Again

The call came unexpected—
they always do. Like starting
to bake a cake… finding out
there's only one egg
when you need two.

"We want to see you again,"
the words biting
like a ripe lemon. "Your
mammogram… doesn't
look quite right."

Damn. The stress.
His fault.
"We want to see you again."
Words better said at
a job interview or from old friends.

When I return
they laminate my aged breast
against cold glass,
scrunch it's white-skin
under radical examination.
A once perky boob, now
compressed and camera-ready.

"Sorry," says the Technician.
"Need to get as close as possible…."
Her yellow teeth and oniony breath
whisper, "Don't move."
My face presses against the metal,
my flattened breast throbs.
One arm against my side
the other strapped to the frigid device.

Pearls Beneath The Rind

She grabs the film, says
she's going to "the back."
Her practiced speech
drones, "It could be worse.
You may need surgery.
Or
we'll see you next year.
Or
in 6-months."

She's being nice, I tell myself.
Pleasant.
I wait and think of him
not thinking of me.

A few minutes later I hear,
"Have a good year."
A long held breath
escapes my mouth.
A storm of relief,
while the blame on him
lays quiet.

Oliver, The Roadrunner

Oliver slams the baby gopher
against the ground.

Whack. Slap. Slap.

Again.

Whack. Slap. Slap.

He skips through brittle sage weeds,
against howling storms
from northern skies.
Oliver's menu is thin this year,
gopher or snake.

He hops across the graveled road
dangling what's left of the rodent.
His headdress bends in the wind
as he scuttles across the field
and out of sight.

Tomorrow, he'll be back to

whack. Slap. Slap.

What I Mean By Rural

Cowboy hats and
snakeskin boots,
pickup trucks
and freight train toots.

Bacon and eggs
whisk through air,
a horse gives birth
to a brand new mare.

Churned butter
and fresh milk,
new born calves
with skins of silk.

School bus drives
in open skies,
dropping farm kids off
to home-made pies.

Revival tents
near stockyard smells,
water witchers hunt
for good water wells.

Holiday parades
march through town,
quiet nights fall
on cultivated ground.

Mason jars
and coffee mugs,
summer humidity
and lots of bugs.

Stacks of straw
and fresh cut hay,
sweet smells of alfalfa
through the day.

Swings on porch
bring neighbors close,
homemade jam
on bread or toast.

Fields of corn,
beans and peas,
county fairs sell
cows that please.

Country smells and
country noise,
make rural "rural"
for farm girls and boys.

New Shoes

My new shoes shined and bent with
ease, conformed
to my feet, I thought.
I stroked their artificial skin.
Their strap laid comfort
across the top of each foot,
arch struck in the right place.
A perfect fit,
I thought.

My big feet were happy.
New shoes now covered my
calluses and blisters,
years of wearing
the wrong shoes
the wrong sizes.
Years of making wrong decisions.

Up and down
the store aisle, checking the low
mirrors, making sure
the shoes still flatter.
A gift for my feet, I thought.
A gift to make
me whole again.

But the next day
when I tried them on,
outside the store,
in sunshine's real light;
outside in the world
where nations didn't agree,
outside, in this light,
my new shoes didn't fit
anymore.

Shoe Stages

It all began with Pappagallos.
They were fashionable, chic,
and expensive.
That was before I knew about
flat sandals and comfort—
before I paid my own way.

When I lived by myself
and worked 9-5
I wore plain pumps—the cheap kind.
The ones that squeaked when
trudging on tiled floors.
I was never one for spikes, heeled sandals
or platforms.
My feet were too uneven,
my head filled with lopsided thoughts,
my heart not into designer things.

I'd think about my Pappagallos—
if the younger crowd
still cared about them,
still yearned to wear its name
around their soft-skinned feet.

Today I live in old lady shoes—
ballet and padded orthopedic flats.
I sometimes wonder
where my hand-me-down Pappagallos are,
if they're helping others navigate
through life's shoe stages.

Can't Go Home No More

Towel rack, flour sack
plastic pipe and kitchen hose
horseweed hardy and still grows.
Dog pens and animal traps
flowers once alive with sap.

Tire gauge, car fenders
dogs chained to dying trees,
garbage entwined with rotting leaves.
Long ago, this was my home,
fields and fields of grassy loam.

Extension cord, car keys
scrap wood where termites dwell,
rubber tire and bicycle bell.
Weathered, wooden beams in fields
where cows once roamed and ate their meals.

Satellite dish, electric lights
lawn mower exposed to dust
fencing reddened, encased with rust.
Kerosene lamps used for lighting,
grayed, faded, whitewashed house siding.

Dawn opens to sunlight's muse
trees tall, twinkle, on white spruce.
Bits and pieces from the farm,
belonged to fields now long gone.

Floyd, Eugene, Clyde and Homer
still hope for fields of soy and clover.
Rose of Sharon bends from force
her dying anger shares remorse.

Can't Go Home No More (continued)

Duck decoys, fishing reel,
wash hangs from withered string
who knew then what life would bring.
The land, unfaithful, like before,
I try, but can't go home no more.

Life Is Bubble Gum Without The Wrapper

Time stretches like bubble gum,
runs through fields of candied hope
or dries like hard taffy.
It jogs through crowds of yesterdays
waving a dozen roses
or wears black and smells of damp earth.
It sings with a sweet lavender voice or
echoes like bullfrogs in a canyon void.
It can fly like a raven between layers of sky,
sing like a crazed Katydid
or wait for limestone to cure.
Time tattoos into our skin as we hang on,
trying to stop
that one last pop.

Eating Worms

The word Failure
flaps across the sky like a banner
again and again,
like a neon sign flashing along
Times Square or a
tickertape parade down Fifth Avenue.

"FAILURE. FAILURE."

It dwells deep in my brain
makes its way into my
digestive tract where clumps of words
thicken. Those jarring letters
keep blinking,
their echoes boom
through the Grand Canyon—
I know it.

"FAILURE. FAILURE."

Another rejection
another "No!"
A perpetual roll around the hamster's wheel
getting nowhere
and anyway
where was I headed?

A slap in the face, a chord
off key. Like broken glass,
chards of metal pound
against my chest.
"Failure" is etched across my brow.
I'm an outcast, an outsider, a loser.
Go ahead, make fun,
put me down, say
those words again and again,

Eating Worms (continued)

"FAILURE. FAILURE."

I hang my sign:
Out to lunch
Gone fishing
Don't bother me

I'm busy… eating worms.

I Don't Want To Die In Chino Valley

Amidst the scrub, and sagebrush,
along barren fields that cry for water.
Where moonbeams breathe down on
scorpion, snake, and centipede, and where
new beginnings desired rural life.

I don't want to die in Chino Valley.
As roadrunner slaps prey against the soft
white flurries of winter, or in summer,
when gopher plays hide-n-seek, and
land gives nothing back but a pregnant beetle.

I don't want to die in Chino Valley. Anytime.
Where dreams tear at couples' souls,
with regrets of why did we move here?
Whose dream was it? Anyway.

I don't want to die in Chino Valley.
Alone.

NIGHTSONGS

Nightsongs 1–Triptych For The Messenger

It was a dream.
I mean the dream
was a dream
if you know what I mean.
I mean the yielding
to the dream that was a
dream. And the feeling
of the dream that was still
another dream.

Strutting in senior high, I wore
a mellifluous ease of motion.
I could play the game, I could
not play the game.
I could game the game.
Act two and final,
at the home of my
principal rival: a Heracles
dressed like the sister.
There was a lover, a quarrel
and a third friend.
I could handle the triads.
I was up for the tetrads.

I told the story to a friend.
He pushed the pedal
and we soared.
I told it again
to the messenger, who
questioning, made me roar.
And back I fell,
keenly hesitant.

Nightsongs 3–The Older Woman

The crowd I sought
had forked the heart and mind,
could find a pearl beneath
a melon rind.
Their queen, a cougar of the ages,
had done the streets
and left her golden traces.
She was twenty years
my senior, I was
surprisingly eager.

The six of us on settees
on the porch.
Pink and puce soon seasoned
our discourse.
Which is when I summoned up
fierce Hemingway. How had
his Jake so gamely lost his way?
So early had she
drawn away his own:
she favored me,
this lady of high tone.

At dinner now we
slowly take our places.
The lady first
so chic in antique laces.
Quick I act and palm
a seat beside her.
A gigolo would fight me
to bestride her.

Her form and eye
bejewel her carnal throne.
I won't move, no
I won't move.
No mortal man
will shatter our repose.

Nightsongs 6–Again The Mafiosi

We strode through town
together down the way,
Crazy Al, the Luch and Vito too.
Their eyes were hard,
their hair slicked back in waves.
Then appeared Adonis
whose blue limo flamed.
Females dressed for night
in scarlet, black and tight,
raised their arms in wonder,
tossing scented note cards
with their names.

The queen stood high in silence by the gate.
She would pick the Don,
the others would die alone.
Twice more compelling than the night,
the Bug himself had whimpered at first sight.

I glanced about and
shuddered at my fate.
Adonis fired back.

My knotted calf it pained.

Big Marv who grew
the curly golden waves.
He roamed the streets
from dusk. He was down
and bad, good with a blade.
They followed him, *les femmes*,
they could never get enough.

He lay the weed on me
one day, back behind
the bunks in the woods
where no one looks.
He stuck it between my lips
and with a grin said:
"Even girls with frills
will bend your way.
Son, ditch the wonk and naysay,
this is the stuff."

For a month I
puffed it in and swore:
"I hadn't tried weed before."
Like a hurler on the mound,
I'd chew it too and frown, then
spit it on the ground.
(For years I'd searched around.)
Cool Marv, he always knew the score.

But his mojo didn't smooth
it out for me.
I gagged and choked,
smelled worse than a skunk.
Having weed in my mouth
was just plain ugly.

So just before the break
of day I woke,
and watched Big Marv
perish in his smoke.

ACKNOWLEDGMENTS

We want to thank our editors, Jim Natal and Elizabeth Rees, for their time and contributions in keeping us on track with this book.

Additionally, Richard would like to thank Carlos Da Rosa for expanding our thoughts about publishing. Carole would like to thank her critique group: Elaine Jordan, Leota Hoover, Colette Ward, Vicky Young, Gretchen Brinck, Carrie Malinowski and Ben Bakke, who passed away in May, 2013, for their continued help and support. Special thanks also goes to the Poetry Cooperative in Prescott, AZ.

The following poems have been published or recognized:
Can't Go Home No More, Yavapai College, *Threshold: Creative Arts Magazine*. Prescott: Yavapai College, 2006. Print. *I Don't Want To Die In Chino Valley*, Yavapai College, *Threshold: Creative Arts Magazine*. Prescott: Yavapai College, 2009. Print. *Next Meal*, Shorb, Terril L. and Schnoeker-Shorb, Yvette A., eds. *What's Nature Got To Do with Me? STAYING Wildly Sane IN A MAD WORLD*. Prescott: Native West Press, 2011. Print. *Sweet Sixteen*, Oregon State Poetry Association Poetry Contest, Fall 2010. Honorable mention for Traditional Verse. *What I Mean By Rural*, Lady Mathers, ed. *Monsoon Magazine's* Poet's Corner, July, 2009.

AUTHORS BIOGRAPHIES

Richard Seldin is a freelance writer who lives with his wife in Bethesda, Maryland. His publications include short fiction and non-fiction in both English and Chinese and translations into English of Chinese novellas and short stories. For many years he worked as an attorney for the United States Government, specializing in International Relations and Trade.

Carole R Seldin-Bolinski (aka CR) has published mystery short stories, flash fiction and poetry. Her poetry credits include winning the Oregon State Poetry Association's new poet's category for *The Car*. She's also a participant in "The Mad Women Poets of Prescott;" a group of local poets who recite their poems at various locations. Bolinski has an M.A. in art education, an M.Ed. in secondary education and has completed the creative writing certificate program at Yavapai College.

COMING SOON

"I Don't Want To Die In
Chino Valley"

Poems by
CR Seldin-Bolinski

CPSIA information can be obtained at www.ICGtesting.com
Printed in the USA
BVOW02s2224180214

345313BV00008B/223/P